I DON'T CARE!

THE ART OF DIVINE INDIFFERENCE

IRENE BRANKIN

Author of *The Visible Woman – More Lust, Less Must*

Throughout this book I have included exercises at the end of each chapter. These are also available as audio files on my website at www.thevisiblewoman.com/recordings

I'd like to offer my thanks to –

My husband Eddie – once again, for his patience
and making the meals while I've been on
the computer.

My son and daughter-in-law, Ian and Louise, and
my lovely grandchildren – Lydia and Harry.

My brother Harry, Jean and family.

The friends who have shared my laughter and tears,
struggles and successes over the years particularly
Anne, Sharon, Kristina, Kirsten, Liz and Jane – I
am grateful to you all.

Once again to all my ex-colleagues and the Board at
The Psychosynthesis & Education Trust, London
and the Psykosyntesakademin in Stockholm.

To all my old and new clients, supervisees and
workshop attendees – in particular, the wonderful
Swedish people who have been part of my life and
always supportive. Here I want to mention in
particular, Nina-Christina Ericsdotter.

My lovely Facebook friends who have supported,
shared and liked my 'stuff'.

My Zumba and HITS friends, particularly Jackie
'Zumba' Bentley who puts up with me attempting to
get fit, and my 'Fat Club' friends who still share
their laughter with me.

I can't thank Michael Mentessi enough for his help, kindness and support with my MP3s, and for starting the Leigh Meetup Group who I feel are now my community – Zoe, Ian, Mike, Yvie, Rich, Gary, Zodie, Suzi, Sally … And particularly Laura, who has been so helpful and supportive with her clarity and who makes me laugh.

To my Virtual Assistant, Sarah Begley, for hanging-on in there while I go a tad crazy at anything to do with Social Media.

To Diana Whitmore, Jackie Walker and Suzy Greaves for taking the time and trouble to give me comments for the book cover.

My grateful thanks go to Lynn Batten for her deep insights and intuitive handling of the book's concepts, and to The Write Factor for their support, patience and advice through the publishing process – Lorna you are a star.

And lastly, thanks go to those who took part in my Survey and to those who agreed to give me their stories even though I did not publish them all. I appreciated your willingness to share.

CONTENTS

FOREWORD   WHISPERS OF THE SOUL   1
INTRODUCTION   THE CAGED TIGER   5
CHAPTER 1   I CARE   11
CHAPTER 2   I OVER-CARE   29
CHAPTER 3   I BURN-OUT   47
CHAPTER 4   STOP   65
CHAPTER 5   CARE LESS   85
CHAPTER 6   CARE FREE   105

FOREWORD

WHISPERS OF THE SOUL

My aim in writing this book is to share my personal and professional experiences in order to help women lead more creative and fulfilling lives, and in doing so, to learn how to recognise when our own needs and desires need to be given priority over other people's needs and desires; and to banish once and for all those feelings of guilt about what we feel we *ought* to be doing instead of what we *want* to be doing. The journey is not an easy one but through listening to our innate wisdom – to what I call the 'whispers of the soul' – we can all begin to live this one precious life more fully.

We are so conditioned by societal norms that many women lose track of the things that once motivated and inspired them. We feel trapped and unable to create the future we desire. Very often these feelings of frustration manifest around middle age, either when the children have flown the nest or when life can seem nothing more than dreary routine and we have forgotten the essence of who we really are.

Having experienced some of these issues myself, I understand exactly how it feels to struggle with the challenges that, from mid-life onwards, we are compelled to wrestle with. Having the courage to make the changes I advocate in this book carries with it the seeds of opportunity and potential – and the possibility of a whole new beginning. Unfortunately however, the sentiment of many women regarding these mid-life changes is predominately one of loss; a perception that the best is over and it's all downhill from here.

In grieving for lost youth, lost looks, missed opportunities, relationship changes and absent children, the outlook appears bleak, the prognosis bland at best. Sadly, this futile yearning for the past not only causes a distress that can spiral downwards into depression, but blocks positive progress into a fulfilling future. We are the ones who can make the changes that we want to see in our lives – no one else can do it for us, so we need to start right now – TODAY! Be the change that you want to see in your life.

I Don't Care! Is actually a book for women of all ages – because it will help you to recognise and avoid the behavioural patterns that can often lead to the creation of your very own personal cage; it is about learning how to put yourself and your needs first; it's about breaking the chains that bind you to a life you no longer find fulfilling. Ultimately, the purpose of this book is to release the 'caged tiger' within you before your symptomatic and desperate roaring gains precedence. This book will show you how to allow yourself the freedom to fulfil your true potential through reconnecting with yourself and the world.

4

INTRODUCTION
THE CAGED TIGER

To all those women who know in their hearts that life is slowly passing them by and that their dreams are being forgotten, if they have not already died – "Wake Up!" Do you want to look back and see that you lived a comfortable but unremarkable life lived in the middle lane, or a life that was lived with vitality, courage and acceptance of uncertainty? Do you want to recall a life filled with a fantastic rollercoaster of experiences, or one of grey mundanity? The choice is yours – but remember this: when you give-in to your true self, you are at last, open and ready to receive the incredible gifts and marvels that lay waiting just for you.

As a psychologist, I have worked with men and women of all ages, although my focus is now on the countless women in mid-to later life who have spent many years caring for others: women who have donned the mantle dictated by our cultural mores so completely that they have all but forgotten who they are or how it is to be truly inspired and motivated.

These women are like caged tigers, trapped in routine and hide-bound by the mundane – even if they are in a high-powered job – whilst inside them the tiger is roaring, "Let me out!" The irony is that this caged tiger of theirs inhabits a self-imposed cage, the bars of which were constructed from years of listening to the carping constraints of an inner voice that is often not even their own. The door of the cage is wide open – but until the inner critic is silenced, stepping across the threshold of the cage is all but impossible.

"I would never speak to anyone the way my inner voice speaks to me!"
CHERRY OCTAVE, WRITER

The caged tiger manifests dis-ease and unhappiness in many ways: depression, obesity, any of the myriad addictions of modern life, anxiety, anger and controlling behaviour being some of the more recognisable symptoms. The tiger's cage may be gilded, beautifully appointed and very comfortable – as many women pour their creativity into making theirs the best cage ever – but it is a cage nonetheless; confining, a prison. The tiger, desperate for escape, paces up and down behind bars of guilt and fear.

The caged tiger is a part of all of us – our individual spirit quashed by societal norms and expectations – therefore, it takes courage to say, "I don't care anymore". How many times in your life have you done something because you felt you ought to, when really you couldn't care less? Like me, I'm sure it's many times. But when the strength is found to throw off years of oppressive expectation, an enormous amount of energy is unleashed.

It is time to wake-up and live your one precious life!

This book will help you to recognise those moments when it's time to say, "I don't care!" and will guide you in how to focus that released energy on the things that are truly important to you, because it is time to wake-up and live your one precious life! Take a good, hard look at yourself. Whose shoes are you actually walking in, and in whose footsteps are you following? I want you to learn how to be comfortable in your own shoes and how to release your latent, powerful energy within.

I Don't Care Is all about helping women to reconnect with their deeper passions and motivations, it's about facilitating an awareness that ultimately, our first responsibility is for our own happiness – because unless we are truly happy in our own skin, we cannot serve our higher purpose in life.

For many women it is incredibly daunting to admit that they don't really care about the things that they have spent a lifetime doing, and yet it is the first step towards liberating the tiger. Most of us spend our lives caring about things that don't really matter and we forget about our dreams – but the key to unlocking the cage is the ability to differentiate between what really matters to you and that which you think *ought* to matter. Our caged tiger is telling us to let it roar, to use its energy and give ourselves the freedom to be visible to the world.

Unless we are truly happy in our own skin, we cannot serve our higher purpose in life.

The sooner we give in to our roar of "I Don't Care!" the better, because then we are free to choose. When we have a choice, our caring will come from a place of love not duty. Our caged tiger is telling us to let it roar, to use its energy and give ourselves the freedom to be visible to the world.

CHAPTER ONE
I CARE

"Care about what other people think and you will always be their prisoner."

– LAO TZU

"I don't care!" – how does it feel to read or say that? When did you last say that? How many times have you muttered to yourself under your breath, "I don't care!" but continued on as if you do?

It is a given in adult life that we should care for each other and the world in all its complexity. There is, after all, so much to care about: not only are there personal and societal concerns about how we are perceived by others and what other people will think of us or say about us if we do or do not comply with these norms, but in this era of global communication and twenty-four hour news coverage, it seems we must care about the state of the world, the economy, the environment, the polar bears, the poor and starving on various continents and the endless suffering caused by global conflicts and disasters too. Australian philosopher Glenn Albrecht has even coined a neologism for the mental distress of caring too much about environmental issues: *solastalgia* – and more and more people are suffering from it.

Yes, there is a lot of caring to do – but is it possible to care too much? Is it possible to negate your concerns in the face of all this overwhelming need, and what exactly would happen if you chose to care less or (gasp) if you chose not to care at all? What would happen if you said, "Enough of all this caring!" – where would the world be if we didn't care? I love this quote from *Eat Pray Love* by Elizabeth Gilbert: "Sit quietly for now and cease your relentless participations. Watch what happens. The birds do not crash out of the sky in mid-flight after all. The trees do not wither and die; the rivers do not run red with blood. Life continues to go on." If you substitute 'relentless participations' with relentless 'caring' the outcome is the same.

In response to a brief survey asking questions based around caring, I found, unsurprisingly, that learning to care comes in the first instance from our home environment through our parents – our carers. Most parents demonstrate their care for us in myriad ways: they feed us and keep us warm; love us and teach us right from wrong. In the precious years between birth and seven years old when we learn the fundamental principles that steer our life's course, we realise that adults care about many things, and we begin to follow this example by caring about these things too. Our parents and society give out constant subtle and not so subtle reminders that we must care.

The very young have a deep need for rules and structure; this is what gives shape to the world and provides meaning and security. Indeed, a large dollop of order is essential for children, all of whom will constantly 'push the envelope' in order to test the boundaries of their existence. I have seen the detrimental effects on clients in later life who have had either too little guidance in childhood or who were over-controlled.

When there are no boundaries, then there's no safety net for children. They need to have something to hit up against which says, "This far and no further". Without boundaries, some children may grow up caring only for themselves and blaming everyone and everything else when things don't go their way. They often end up displaying appalling behaviour, due to their unrealistic sense of entitlement, and then wonder why they are not successful in life.

A friend of mine shared with me her experience of having her granddaughter –who she loved dearly – to stay at her house. Other than ending up absolutely exhausted after every visit, she was intrigued to see how the child's behaviour became what can only be described as obnoxious during these stays. My friend talked to her daughter about this and they agreed a plan of action to address the behaviour, but it seemed things just got worse whatever they did. It turned out, after much discussion that the issue was with the parents saying "No" and sticking to that decision. However, my friend worked with them to explain why it is so important to give a child boundaries, and so the parents agreed to do that, however hard it seemed. The result was that their daughter's behaviour did improve, and although she would still be naughty, she was aware of the boundaries – she knew that she could go so far and no further. She knew that she was loved and eventually realised that it was her behaviour that was causing problems. In due course, after this realisation dawned on her, she began to behave in a way that no longer caused tension in the family.

Another example may be when children do what they are told at school and are very good in class, then play up badly when they arrive home.

So, as children, we quickly learn the benefits of socialisation – we crave praise and love from adults – we know that if we behave well we are rewarded with love and affection or even food, treats or toys; other children like us if we are nice to them, and we are included in game playing and social situations, and at school we learn to do as we are told and to care for others – be it through the annual ritual of Children In Need, or fundraising for those less well off than ourselves. Ultimately, from a very young age, we learn that there are significant advantages to being liked by both adults and our peers, and we care about that. Essentially, most of us would rather be on the inside than the outside – we'd rather be included than excluded and to be included we have to be nice, to care, to behave ourselves and do as we are told.

We also learn that we can be punished if we don't care and don't obey the rules, and this is not so nice, as any two-year-old on the naughty step will tell you – so we begin to learn to adapt our behaviour accordingly, drawing on the examples we hear, see and unconsciously sense from the culture and environment in which we live. A two-year-old, red faced and screaming with rage as she hurls herself against the strictures and boundaries of acceptable behaviour, exemplifies how the foundations of the cage that will eventually trap the tiger are laid. I am not advocating a lawless and anarchic childhood: all of us understand that the cocoon of childhood woven by caring parents and a society that, by and large, adheres to the same framework of care, gives a child the necessary security to deal with the messy chaos of adult life. This book is not about the abnegation of all responsibility however attractive an idea! The example serves only to point out how, very early in life, we may start to lock ourselves into our personal cage. "Be nice," we tell our children, "share, care, and be good. Help each other and be kind." Undoubtedly, all of these things are good in and of themselves, and benefit society as a whole – yet all of these things can create the bars of a cage if we leave no room for ourselves and our own needs.

When a child is made to feel that their anger is somehow 'bad' this is often internalised and the child comes to believe that rather than the behaviour being unacceptable it is in fact he or she that is intrinsically bad or naughty. As the child matures and the suppressed and internalised anger surfaces as it inevitably does, it has become warped by pressure and constriction and is likely to manifest through more socially acceptable forms of expression such as criticism, spiteful sarcasm, a tendency to over control the behaviour of others, a victim mentality or it may even manifest as illness.

Many children live with the notion that if they were 'a better person' the anger and tension in the family home would disappear: a child is the centre of its own little universe, believing therefore that everything that happens in that universe must in some way be attributable to their actions. Because of this perception, children will often blame themselves for trouble in the home and as a result become self-hating and begin to act out in various ways – perhaps playing the clown, or possibly becoming moody and difficult – to release or deflect emotional tensions within the family.

Does this sound familiar to you? Did you internalise your parents' stress levels? Did you look after your siblings to please your mother because she was always so busy or tired? Are you beginning to recognise the bars of your cage that were constructed in your childhood? Sadly, during our childhood it would seem that we are not given much, if any, instruction that it is just as important to care for and nurture ourselves, as it is to care for others.

Most of us grow up within a family feeling that it is safe to love, to fight, to argue and then to make amends, and we trust that despite our behaviour it is unlikely that we will be excluded, *because we are loved*. We come into the world deeply open and receptive to our carers: we are loved and in turn we love. It is a matter of survival – we bond or we die. Our parents and families are the mirrors and vehicles through which we learn to see ourselves. Many of us spend a lifetime trying to gain our parents' blessing or approval – or for the unlucky, a lifetime in therapy trying to step back from their values. Eventually though, we all have to take responsibility for who we are and what we do with our lives. We can blame everything we don't like in ourselves or in our lives on our parents and our upbringing until the cows come home, but in the end, the only person who can change your life is you.

It is just as important to care for and nurture ourselves as it is to care for others.

Have you ever had that two-year-old's desire to stamp your feet and shout, "I don't care!" whilst in reality you are standing with glazed eyes and a fixed smile on your face listening to someone's tale of woe? How many times have you dropped everything to run to the aid of someone whose drama is always more important than your own plans? Are you one of those friends who automatically prioritises other people's needs above your own? Why can't you say "No" and stick to it?

Try to listen to your inner voice, the one that eventually takes over from the homogenous, internalised nagging voice of your parents, siblings and anyone else who had any authority in your childhood, many of whom were probably judgmental or critical. Just think about it. How do you talk to yourself if you've not done as well as expected, or look as good as you could? Harsh or what?

It is important to point out at this juncture, the difference between your 'inner voice' and your 'inner critic'. The inner critic is usually motivated by fear and it's the voice we take on from childhood whether from parents, school or society. It is the echo of our parental voice that tells us what we can or can't do; that says, (if your parenting was poor), "You'll never be able to do that," or "Who do you think you are?" "It's much easier to not bother than try and fail," or even, "You're useless, you're good for nothing..."

In many instances, the inner critic is so strong that it can come in and try to override one's true inner voice – your own deeply-held wisdom that is often difficult to access in the maelstrom of modern life. The inner critic is often in dispute with this deeper inner knowing, and will try to keep you 'safe' and under control (as our parents once did), but it doesn't recognise that you are an evolving, growing and changing being – and one that can now make your own decisions. The inner critic is one of the most challenging obstacles for us to gain freedom from – it expresses itself as a kind of self-sabotage, but it has been going on for so long, that many women do not even know of its existence.

This inner critic can block us from having the freedom to choose. It is so much a part of us, that we think it *is* us – rather than an echo of other people's opinions and judgments. The boundaries our parents lay down for us as children were appropriate and necessary then, but as we evolve and grow into adulthood, we are able to make our own decisions and value judgments. This hangover from childhood is something many people, not just women, find difficult to let go of. You are not your parents, you are your own person!

The inner voice comes from the heart; it is your gut instinct, your feelings and your intuition. It is the whispers of your soul speaking through your heart. The inner voice tends to speak through our body, not through our thoughts. You know when a decision just feels right? When you feel that excitement in your stomach; when you know it is the right direction you're going in; when you trust your decisions – this is your Wise Woman talking to you (your inner voice of wisdom). She can also communicate in symbols, songs, books and other methods.

She speaks to you when you're afraid or when you're upset or exhausted, by comforting you. When you feel good about yourself, when you give yourself a pat on the back, when a smile comes to your lips, when your heart is full of love, this is your inner voice – your Wise Woman – at work. Your inner voice doesn't judge you – she's on your side and encourages you – and helps you to become more calm and comfortable with yourself.

In summary, your Inner Critic is the personification of fear and tells you you'll never make it, you're hopeless, too stupid, ugly... Your Inner Voice is the personification of love – it makes you laugh, inspires you; it believes in you, delights in you, encourages and enables you to be calm when chaos reigns, and soothes you amidst the storms of life.

Your inner critic can make you fearful to try anything new and be overly anxious about what others think of you. This state of constant self-disapproval can lead to expecting too much of yourself: this is self-denigration, a self-putdown where you are constantly berating yourself for doing nothing about your life or your aspirations. You've had so much criticism in your life that you don't try anything new because of fear you will get it wrong, and you won't be good enough. The internalised message is, "Don't rock the boat, keep quiet – maintain the status quo!"

It's okay not to be perfect – it's fine to feel confused and insecure.

But, repression is not healthy. Everyone needs to express that which longs for recognition – the deep feelings that need to be heard. Until these feelings are acknowledged the anger and pain will continue. It's hard to own-up to anger because anger however justified is often perceived by others as irrational or out of control behaviour, but most commonly the underlying cause of anger is pain. The important thing is to understand that it's okay not to be perfect – it's fine to feel confused and insecure. Until we acknowledge these feeling and allow them expression, we will never escape the cage. Great insights into who we are and what makes us tick can be gleaned from our insecurities and even from depression. Once we find and express our inner voice, these feelings will begin to lose their destructive power.

We all need to find our inner voice – the one that doesn't undermine, but encourages positive growth towards real self-acceptance. Once we recognise that inner voice and learn to accept what it is saying and take action to align our lives with what it is telling us, then we have the emotional equivalent of a hacksaw and are ready to begin work on the bars of the cage.

It is important to recognise when your inner critic is dominating and tell it to go away – it's one finger up to sky time and a firm, "I don't need you!" Try to simultaneously distract yourself with something that forces the voice to stop even for a moment, for example looking at your watch, checking your text messages or doing some stretching exercises – anything that breaks the concentration on that critical voice. Think of someone or something that makes you feel good inside or puts a smile on your face, and then use that picture whenever your inner critic is nagging on at you. Challenge the negative thoughts by reframing them: "You'll never do it," becomes "I admire my courage for trying new things." Take some deep, calming breaths and smile at the words you are saying to yourself – that way, the negative words will lose their power and the positive words will become more emphasised.

It is true that most of us are afraid of the caged tiger; the pent-up rage that we know is in there, lurking beneath the ready smile and warm embrace. This rage that can cause problems for our bodies, because anger and stress release the 'fight or flight' hormones that take a toll our wellbeing. Unresolved anger is toxic – it can destroy both spirit and self – it's a killer, because it can literally murder your soul!

How did it come to this? When did the world decide that just because you are a good, caring person it means that you must always be ready to listen, always available to help out anywhere, any time? "Do I," you might ask yourself, "do I walk around with an indelible mark on my forehead signifying that I am a 'mug'? Is there a sign saying 'PUSHOVER' writ large in neon lights over my head?"

Listen... this may come as a shock to you – you may not at this point even believe it's possible – but I am telling you that you don't have to be that person anymore, because you have a *choice*. You can decide that your life matters and then you can learn to say, "No". You can say to that friend who is always in some kind of mess "NO MORE! I've heard your stories and your dramas time and time again, and now it's time for you to do something about your life." Or simply, "Sorry, I've got no time – must dash," or even, "Sounds tough..." put a sympathetic hand on the shoulder and then just leave. Yes, that's right! Walk away and keep on putting one foot in front of the other, and there you are… You've moved on – you've started to break down the barriers of your cage. It's not easy – it takes courage to do this – but it is possible. Do not be afraid to say "No".

Change your perception of yourself and this will change how others perceive you.

The bottom line, harsh and unpalatable though it may be, is that you have allowed this to happen to you. Your indecisiveness, timidity and fear, your need to be seen as a *nice* woman can be sensed; picked up in your body language and in the tone of your voice. This does not have to be the case. You can change your perception of yourself and this in turn will change how others perceive you. You do not have to care to the point of altering your plans and appointments for the entire day because your friend will be a bit peeved if you do not go shopping with her on Tuesday. You do not have to worry as to why you weren't asked to lunch when others were invited. Maybe it was simply assumed you were too busy! Not everything in life and every reaction from others is down to what you may or may not have done. You can just dismiss this kind of interaction. These things are not life threatening, and if they have any meaning at all it will become apparent, so in the meantime you can say, "So what?"

Try it … think of one thing that has been playing on your mind. It might be a conversation or a job undone, a missed appointment – anything at all that's currently bothering you. Now repeat after me, "SO WHAT?"

Stop it! Stop all the unnecessary emotional angst, stop the toadying and the placating, stop the pandering and the non-essential ministering-to. Stop giving a toss what your neighbours said about you putting out the weekly rubbish collection in your dressing gown. What is it to you what they think? By the way, I am talking about myself here! Stop minding so much: stop worrying about the opinion of people who don't matter, and the people whose opinions do matter will have more respect for you. Stop being afraid is what I am saying in this book. It's time to change the neon sign to 'I Don't Care' until you are ready to change it to 'I care deeply when I want to'.

You can choose to give yourself what you have given to others for years: time, compassion, attention and love.

You behaved as you did in the past – that was then – but now you have a choice. You do not HAVE to do anything about your life: there is no OUGHT to, but if you are reading this book it is because you feel a pressing need within yourself to acknowledge your own desires. You *can* choose to give yourself what you have given to others for years: time, compassion, attention and love. Learn to value yourself and your time, and others will follow suit.

EXERCISE

Imagine your Caged Tiger pacing up and down, with all the energy internalised and the emotional charge filling the cage. Sometimes the tiger is sleeping in the corner, but always just waiting and waiting. What would your response to the tiger be?

Now imagine that you are the tiger and the tiger is you. What are you doing? What is happening in your body? What is happening in your mind? How do you feel?

Take your time, go deep inside your tiger and experience everything – shy away from nothing. When you return to yourself, write down your responses to the questions in this exercise with complete honesty.

It is very important for you to listen to the tiger – it is time you did.

CHAPTER TWO
I OVER-CARE

"Givers must set limits as takers rarely do."
- IRMA KURTZ

Given all that we learn and take on board in childhood, it is hardly surprising that many of us begin to 'over-care' in adulthood. We become so concerned with the reactions and perceptions of others about our way of being, that we lose sight of our true selves. It has been ingrained in us from an early age that the 'sharing, caring society' that most of us want to see as a working reality depends largely on the caring aspect; this means that many of our own impulses and predilections are constantly being tempered if not subsumed into the amorphous greater good.

Of course, we cannot blindly follow our own pleasures and desires whatever they may be, as this leads to addictive and self-destructive behaviour, which one look at Western culture nowadays all too obviously confirms, when we pursue the path of doing only "what I want". However, purely dutiful over-caring and the subsequent denial of our own inner needs can be as detrimental to health and

happiness as the unbridled selfishness of hedonism.
The key, as in all things, is balance.

We do not want to be judged and found wanting
and so we demonstrate what good carers we are at
the expense our true feelings and by muffling our
inner voice – because we are afraid: our fear is that
the world will close ranks against us and we will
become isolated, that we will be ridiculed and
disparaged, or made to feel ashamed because we
don't care enough. Digging our heels in and saying
"NO!" becomes impossible, even when our inner
voice protests loudly that it does not want or care to
do or think or be whatever is currently being asked
of us. The overriding emotions that we experience
when we do not comply with a request or an
expectation are feelings of guilt and shame, and for
most of us these are very uncomfortable emotions,
so we avoid creating them as much as possible.

This was the case with Anne, who came to me at a
time in her life where she felt she had no personal
choices left to her and although she was resigned to
the treadmill of her life, she also felt overwhelmed
and lost in the despair of an existence that felt
pointless and unfulfilling. Over time she came to
the understanding that her over-caring had led her
to this point, and she was able to realise that her
entire identity had been built around this caring
persona. She told me, "It's been a real battle to let
go of over-caring: my perception of myself was so
bound up in that role that I lost my own inner
direction. I worked hard out of a misplaced sense of

duty over things that others got the credit for and I allowed myself to believe that this was how life worked. As a consequence I was always tired and unmotivated. I lived my life like a robot, just going through the motions." It took a long time for Anne to acknowledge that her over-developed sense of duty – her moral conscience – led her to put the needs of others before herself, to the detriment of her own life. This is still something she is struggling with. The journey can be long and arduous, but it is definitely worth taking.

I think it is important here to differentiate between having what is euphemistically known as a 'conscience' and the kind of self-abnegation that leads to the despairing roar of the caged tiger. Of course, it is healthy to care about others and most of us know when we have been a bit selfish: when we've gone too far in the opposite direction and been unkind, unfair or thoughtless. We know when we are in the wrong and usually we can admit it, apologise and hopefully make amends – this is just the stuff of life, the wear and tear of human existence. Everybody experiences times when it is fundamentally important for our own needs to take a back seat and lend help and support to others, just as there are times when if you didn't step-up you would not like yourself very much. This is not what this book is about: I am not suggesting for one moment that you should become an unfeeling and self-absorbed egomaniac, in the name of your personal freedom! This will not benefit you anymore than caring too much does, but in the interests of balance, and personal integrity there must be the recognition that your needs are as important as everyone else's. The fact that you are reading this book is a good sign; it means that you have begun to recognise that you count.

There must be a recognition that your needs are as important as everyone else's.

This is about YOU. It has to be about you now because the tiger says so – but this is about the *true* you. So how are YOU feeling? We are not talking about your friends and family and how they are feeling about you; we are not talking about your neighbours or colleagues and how you think you ought or should be relating to them; and we are not talking about the world at large and all the neediness in it … What we are talking about is YOU. We are exploring who you are and how you are and what it is that you truly care about.

EXERCISE

A good place to start is to make a regular practice of stillness. Find a quiet place where you will not be disturbed and can simply be still. Make sure that you are warm enough and that your body is comfortable – you can sit in a chair or lie down – whatever you feel most comfortable with. If you choose to be outside, if possible be somewhere where the sounds that you hear are from nature. Close your eyes and focus on your breathing, slowing it down. When your breathing has become regular and even, take a deep breath in through your nose and let it out slowly and steadily through your mouth, do this three times, breathing in more deeply with each inhalation.

Now imagine that you are surrounded by a soft, white light. It is as pervasive as the air and as you breathe in air you are also breathing in the light which is suffusing your body. Breathe in the light right down to your toes: push it out into the tips of your fingers and up to the top of your head. As you exhale, release any tension you may be feeling – you can imagine your tensions as colours: what colour are yours? Breathe in the light, exhale the tension … Breathe in the light, exhale the tension … Breathe in the light, exhale the tension.

Listen to your body – it will tell you where you are holding your tension: is it in your neck and shoulders or your back? Perhaps your stomach is tight or you are unconsciously clenching your teeth? Wherever it is, make a conscious effort to relax those muscles. Tell yourself to trust your own heart and that all is well: you are at one with yourself. Breathe in the light, exhale the tension and find your peace in the here and now.

Try to do this exercise until your body is relaxed and your tensions have melted away. The more often you practice this, the easier it will be to relax and tune-in to your body. If you carve out this special time that is only for you, not only will it help to still the busy buzz of your mind and create a focus on your physical wellbeing, it will also help you to practise the art of making time for yourself and give you the space to begin to consider what it is that YOU need.

The truth of what it is that you need is already inside you. Learn to trust the whispers of your soul as they will guide you and teach you to accept yourself – warts and all. You don't have to continually prove your self-worth by over-caring – instead, start by believing it is possible to be open to what your heart tells you, and inspiration will come from being aligned with your true nature. This is the foundation of real joy and connection; it will serve to enable you to create the future you want.

This time can be a turning point for you, if you choose it to be; a place of beginning where you recognise that things have to be different, and that there are some things and even some people you really couldn't care less about! This fact is absolutely acceptable. I'm saying don't run around wasting your time on people and things you don't care about. Don't waste your energy: focus on who needs to come first – YOU.

If you exercise the prerogative of 'not caring' there is always someone happy to let you know that this is not on, and that there is something wrong with your attitude, your thinking and well ... your very being – so rather than feel ostracised and criticised you strenuously set out to demonstrate your great capacity in the caring department. Rather than face being an outcast in society the tendency is then to over-care. "Here I am," you shout, "always on call, ready and willing to negate myself and put everyone and everything else first." This is done out of compulsion because you feel you *must* behave this way. When you have practised the exercise above a number of times, you may begin to recognise yourself in one of the following scenarios:

THE PEOPLE-PLEASER

This is when the good, understanding person who sees all sides of all problems and who is all things to all people is forced into being. The message 'I must care or I am a bad person' becomes ingrained and "Yes" becomes the automatic response to any request – you may even volunteer for things before ever being asked. The subtext is, "I'll be anyone you want me to be or need me to be as long as you include me." Everybody loves a people-pleaser – after all, when something needs doing, she'll do it! The people-pleaser looks to others to validate her own existence and eventually she can get so good at it she just knows without being asked who or what she has to be and do to gain the approval that she craves. Do you recognise her?

THE MARTYR

Then there is the martyr who won't allow herself to have any fun because there is always something or someone far more important than her own needs. She may even come to enjoy the inverted egoism and masochistic undertones of self-neglect. Are you a bit of martyr? Do you go out of your way to help

someone, then moan constantly about it afterwards?
Do you begrudgingly support and care for others,
but are inwardly seething with resentment and
anxiety? Do you recognise her?

THE MOTHER MARY

Or perhaps you are the archetypal self-sacrificing
mother who can never go anywhere or do anything
outside of the cycle of household drudgery, because
it is washing day or shopping day, or taking the
children swimming day – and of course the family
must come first. Do you try to outdo your sisters or
friends in the 'I'm too good to be true' stakes? Do
you recognise her?

*This is conditioning that is handed down the
generations and is not the kind that gives you good hair!*

When women become mothers this is often the
seedbed for a lifetime of servitude, as the almost
total dedication to another being – which is
absolutely necessary for babies and young children
– becomes, over time, ingrained and
unacknowledged habitual behaviour. When you are
bought up to believe that to be a good person you
must take care of everyone else first, it becomes the
norm that before you can do anything even
remotely self-indulgent, you must make sure that

everyone and everything else has been attended to. I am telling you that this is conditioning that is handed down the generations and is not the kind that gives you good hair!

THE GO-GETTER

But perhaps you are at the other end of the spectrum, a career woman who has sacrificed any aspirations you may have had for a family of your own to the expectations and pressures of a job? You cared more about getting to the top of the ladder than anything else, but now you find that you are clutching the rungs of the ladder in white-knuckled desperation, trying not to lose your balance as you glare resentfully up at the glass ceiling.

Like most women, you probably see a part of yourself in all of these archetypes, trying to balance the impossible; doing everything for everyone and smiling through clenched teeth whilst tensions in the home stretch to breaking point. Whichever route you have taken to get to this point, you are now beginning to acknowledge and resent the fact that you are starting to disappear, as more and more of your life is taken over by other people's needs and criteria. Do you recognise the situations and choices that have led you to create the caged tiger?

S o now you are paying some attention to the fact that the things *you* want to do are consistently shifted to the back burner, but even if the opportunity arises to indulge in something for yourself, you are so exhausted from dancing to so many different tunes that you never have the energy to go for it anyway and you tell yourself that it doesn't matter, that it's not important. Effectively you are telling yourself that you don't matter because you are not important. This inner critic is helping to keep you in your cage, but however gilded it may be, it is still a prison. Your critical self discourages you and keeps you thinking narrowly, leading you in some ways to expect too little of yourself and others and to expect far too much in other ways.

This discouraging inner dialogue will make you fearful and keep you in your place; it will tell you that you are too tired, too out of practice, too fat, too thin, too old and too boring. It will tell you not to rock the boat and to know your place. Consequently, you will not be inclined to venture out of your comfort zone, preferring to stay within self-imposed parameters and whilst you may have everything that you think you need within the cage, indeed everything that you thought you ever wanted – a family, a career, friends etc – something is not right in your world and you find yourself crying into your breakfast, drinking in the afternoons and having an affair with the postman (maybe not in that order or even those particular things, but you get the drift).

Not content with keeping you in your place, your inner critic will then berate you for your unhappiness citing numerous reasons why you have no right to even this: "You're so lucky, so many people have nothing," etc., and so because you don't deserve the luxury of tears you will pick yourself up, stick that smile back on your face and carry on with your caring.

Women are good at putting themselves down: I'm not good enough, bright enough, pretty enough, talented enough … "I am not enough" is often our mantra. We don't take enough pride in our talents and skills: worrying more about what others think of us; we downplay our unique qualities and often shoot ourselves down in flames before someone else does. But most women have a deep desire to create meaning and purpose in their lives and no one wants to look back on a life full of regrets and unfulfilled potential. Let me remind you at this point of the wise words of the late, great Maya Angelou: "You alone are enough. You have nothing to prove to anybody."

Because you are good at slapping that smile back on your face, nobody sees or knows the pain you are in. You maintain your acceptable persona, you work hard, you do a lot of caring and you do your best to project the image of how you should be: how you think you *ought* to be. You do what is expected of you and if you do very occasionally let your 'roar' out, you cover it quickly and apologise profusely, overcompensating for the bad girl who must not be allowed to exist. Maybe you do a bit more exercise because the endorphins help a bit; maybe you decorate the house over and over, externalising an inner need for change; maybe you go shopping and buy loads of things you don't really need to fill a hole that's getting bigger and bigger no matter how much stuff you try to plug it with? Maybe you double your hours at work in an effort to appease the guilt you feel at your dissatisfaction? Whatever it is that you do, it is only a temporary solution: the pain will be back. The tiger will roar.

Don't let fear rob you of your ability to show the world how talented and gifted you are.

Society projects the notion that women can have it all, in full knowledge that most women will not be allowed to live up to their full creative potential, especially in the job-market where glass ceilings abound. There is still a very long way to go before working mothers will be able to successfully balance a career with home life – if it ever happens. All of which makes taking a leap or even a small step towards change and fulfilment seem very difficult. Women who have had to try to balance home-life and career will understand the frustrations and limitations of both sides of the coin.

Even if you do manage to maintain a job or a career, it is not necessarily fulfilling or even something that you care about, and when you are tired all the time, the thought of affecting any kind of change is overwhelming and exhausting. How do you even know what you want when you are too tired to be bothered to work it out? Life is difficult enough without putting this kind of pressure on yourself, and so it goes on ... These examples of the pressures of modern life include just some of the many factors that can lead to a downward spiral, at times even into the long, slow slide into depression and addiction.

Changing your attitude to life will change your life.

I am saying, don't let fear rob you of your ability to show the world how talented and gifted you are. Don't make yourself deliberately small; celebrate your unique abilities, and remember, we are all here to make a difference in the world – it is your attitude that makes all the difference! Hiding your light under a bushel may mean that you will not be seen to fail but it will also ensure that you will miss out on opportunities and adventures. Fear of success will keep you trapped in the cage and scared of your own life. Many of us are afraid of success because success shines a light on us and we are used to hiding our light. But, as writer Marianne Williamson wrote, "Our deepest fear is not that we are inadequate. Our deepest fear is that we are powerful beyond measure." I am saying, do not be afraid to embrace your power! In doing so you will change your attitude to life and so, will change your life. Ultimately, nothing will change unless change happens.

Try this. Find a quiet space where you can be alone and just let your roar out! Your anger and rage can inspire you to change and it is absolutely possible to turn your fury into a positive force for action. Look at what Bob Geldof achieved with his volcanic rage at the horrors of famine. Turn it outwards and change things for the better. I am not suggesting that you go on an Attila-the-Hun type rampage through your town, creating chaos and wreaking havoc: enjoyable as it might be at the time, ultimately it will not help! But you can put that passion and drive to good use rather than let it give you ill health or a drinking problem. If you use your anger it can give you the courage to see the reality of your life and provide the energy to get on with doing something about it. You owe it to yourself to develop your unique individuality, to listen to your heart and to start to live by your own inner compass. The alternative is a life and an identity overwhelmed by the needs of others and that isn't working for you, is it?

This is the call to change. This is the day you wake up and ask yourself where did I go? Who am I now? Why am I in pain? What am I going to do with the rest of my life?

EXERCISE

Sit down in a quiet place with a notepad and pen and list three things that you feel you should/ought to care about. These can be anything ... they may be people or events or causes. Now search your heart. How do you *actually* feel when you think about these things? What emotions are paramount for each of these things that you are considering? Write them down as they occur.

Is the result of what you feel about the things on your list empowering or disempowering?

Now list three things that you believe you truly care about and do the same.

How much of what you feel is empowering/ disempowering?

If you are conflicted by this exercise, examine that ... Why are you conflicted? What is causing your confusion? Write it down.

How much of what you feel about what is on the lists is the same for both lists?

Now choose the item on your list that has produced the most negative and disempowering emotions and say out loud: "I don't care about ..." Say it very LOUD as many times as you feel you want to.

How do you feel...? Write it down.

Say it again. You are beginning to change the habits of a lifetime, if only for a moment.

CHAPTER THREE
I BURN-OUT

"If you feel burnt-out, if you feel demoralised and exhausted, it is best to withdraw and restore yourself."
– THE DALAI LAMA

I t is totally natural for us to care – we all care, unless there is some kind of unfortunate anomaly in our psychological make-up. Not only is caring important for a healthy emotional life, it is crucial to our survival. Caring is expressed in so many different ways: from meeting the needs of our family by providing food, warmth and shelter, to kind words and loving touch. The sympathetic human touch delivers so much more than meets the eye. There are studies that conclude that babies who are seldom held and who do not experience the loving caresses of a caring parent do not thrive, and although their physical needs are met, they may even die. At the other end of the spectrum are some autistic children who cannot bear to be touched because although the transmission of energy involved may be full of love and compassion, the sensory overload is too much for them to handle.

When we caress a lover the exchange of energies is immediately apparent to the parties involved and conversely, if someone lays rough hands on us the jolt of negative energy that is transmitted is sometimes enough to disable our reactions. All of this information is transmitted simply through the medium of touch; our touch can convey our emotional state better than any amount of words. Ultimately, caring for another sentient being is all about giving and receiving energy – in all its forms. We are all consciously and unconsciously transmitting and receiving energy all the time and without this capacity our lives would be infinitely poorer. However, one's energy can be easily depleted, especially if it is not reciprocated, and this is at the root of burn-out.

So, caring comes naturally to most people, and this innate mechanism is fostered and encouraged in us as we grow through childhood to adulthood. Most of us have been exposed to the creed of caring, and a certain amount of indoctrination as to the behavioural patterns of caring has inevitably been instilled in us from our parents – it is true to say that what our parents were concerned about, we tend to be concerned about. It is usually the case that we care about our loved ones and our friends, animals, and the world around us; about our lives and the lives of those we love; about safe communities, climate change, war zones, traumatised children and famine; about the Euro, the banks and unemployment; about the melting of the polar ice, GM foods, industrial farming and so on and on, *ad infinitum*. As I said in the beginning of this book, there is a lot to care about – overwhelmingly so. But what happens when we start to take our caring far too seriously?

We cannot singlehandedly put the world to rights, however much we want to. Of course this does not mean that we should turn our backs on all the problems of the world we live in, but if we do not get things in perspective and understand what is possible to achieve as an individual, and what is not within our control, then we will spend most of our lives worrying about situations and events that are beyond our individual capacity to change. The Serenity Prayer is worth repeating every day, because it reminds us that we are not personally responsible for all the world's ills:

> *God, grant me the serenity to accept the things I*
> *cannot change,*
> *The courage to change the things I can,*
> *And wisdom to know the difference.*

In an experiment in 1958 published in *Scientific American*, Joseph V Brady used chimpanzees to prove that thinking you might have some control over certain events is more psychologically damaging than knowing that you don't have any control at all! The chimps were given electric shocks every 20 seconds, but one of the chimps was conditioned to press a lever that forestalled the shock *if* the chimp timed it properly. The other chimp had no choice but to endure the situation. The chimp with the lever and therefore with some control proved to be infinitely more stressed in ways that I will not describe here, than the chimp with no such control. I would like to state categorically that I find all such experimentation absolutely abhorrent, nevertheless the experiment has taken place and the results are well documented. I use this example only to illustrate the point that unnecessary and pointless anxiety about things you cannot control causes untold mental and physical ill health.

Of course, we can all do our best to be a responsible member of the human community, but if we labour under the guilt-ridden delusion that we are somehow responsible for the fate of the world (and if that is the case, we definitely need psychological help!) or if we give ourselves the impossible task of ensuring that everyone we love is always happy (or any one of the innumerable permutations of over-caring) then what happens is that we burn-out. Burn-out is caused by our sense of failure and of feeling ashamed that we are unable to attain these goals.

Helplessness and futility in the face of the enormity of all the things we care about inevitably leads to fear: what will happen if my son loses his job? How will my husband cope if I have to go into hospital? Who's going to run the school fete if I don't do it? We also tend to project into scenarios that are always worst case; understandably we do not want to lose our loved ones, our home, our planet, our possessions, etc., and so we try to do it all. We subscribe to Save the Children, (whale, tiger, elephant) because the worst case scenario is extinction, and that would be terrible. We babysit more often for our stressed and overworked family member because we worry that they will become ill. We stay longer at work to make enough money to save for a rainy day – because we really believe there will be one, or that we will end up as a bag lady. Living our lives as if the worst is going to happen, in fear of every terrible thing that might occur and swallowing back our anger depletes our energy on many levels and ultimately leads to burn-out

We give to Sport Relief, Comic Relief, Children In Need, Oxfam, Greenpeace, Christian Aid or any of the other myriad charities doing good work – because we care, we really do. And because after all, we are the lucky ones, the ones that all this awful stuff is not happening to. It is for good reason that the term 'compassion fatigue' or sometimes 'compassion overload' has been coined, because it specifically expresses this overwhelming phenomenon of the times we live in. We just care so damn much about everything.

It is hardly surprising that in the face of all these demands to be, do and give more and more on every front, that anger and resentment begins to percolate in our hearts – slowly and imperceptibly it grows, until our actions become begrudging and bitter, and this in turn leads to the very opposite of all that we are trying to achieve on the caring front. When we are full of resentment at the massive amount of care and support we are expecting from ourselves (and have led everyone else to expect from us), it is extremely difficult if not impossible to actually give to others, because in our hearts and minds we are exhausted by the sheer volume of how much there is to take care of. No wonder there is no energy left at the end of the day; no wonder that there is nothing left for YOU – just overwhelming tiredness.

Yes, YOU who are always at the bottom of the list. YOU who is now feeding your caged tiger with chocolate or alcohol or watching trash TV just to switch off for five minutes. Or, maybe you are reading ridiculous articles about pointless celebrities you have barely heard of because for a few moments you will be distracted from the realisation that you cannot stand what your life has become. If there is no joy and no meaning to be found in the life you are living then no matter how much caring or how much giving you do, it will never provide the fulfilment you really desire, and you will remain stuck in the unrewarding and perpetual cycle of guilt and pain.

Guilt will inform you that you have a good life and no reason to be so ungrateful; futility will whisper that it's better not to listen to your dreams or admit your yearnings because failure is always lurking; and so you close your eyes and ears to possibility and the caged tiger gains strength. Anger and frustration turned inward can do a lot of damage but the ingrained habit of niceness is going to prevent you from expressing yourself. So you hide it as you've always done, you put up the barriers, batten down the hatches and pretend. This in turn means that you withdraw from your true emotions and cut yourself off from your instinctive, intuitive self. You are heading towards burn-out.

Low energy and a feeling of emptiness are symptoms that are often labelled as depression; however I view these symptoms as precursors of change.

It is frightening to just STOP and re-evaluate your life. To face up to who you are and who you've become is scary because you may not like what you see – but if you do not make changes and decide what it is that's *really* important to you, then you may find yourself getting ill and burning-out and actually, having no choice at all. When the overload is too great there may be an involuntary turning away: a day when you simply turn your face to the wall because it is all too overwhelming; a day when you just can't get out of bed; when you cannot face work or even life itself; when you 'pull a sickie' and just hide at home. Have you done that? Because if you have, it may be a sign that you're close to burn-out.

Given all that we have discussed so far, it will come as no surprise that the incidence of burn-out, alcoholism and drug addiction in the caring professions is very high. One report from Holland suggests that as many as 40% of Dutch GPs may experience burn-out during the course of their career. Also at significant risk of burn-out are nurses, social workers and teachers. Burn-out stalks those who care. Alongside the considerable amount of genuine caring that these professions demand, walks the spectre of blame. Society places high expectations on members of these professions and does not seem to afford them the luxury of being human, placing the burden of blame alongside that of caring. And as we already know, caring is *not* easy! Failure is inevitable for many, many people whose jobs and lives are predicated on caring for others, yet failure, far from being seen as the great teacher that it undoubtedly is, has become unacceptable. We cannot be seen to fail, and therefore we soldier on.

We cannot show our vulnerability or else we are not only seen as having something 'not quite right' about us, but get labelled or put in a box marked 'Problem'. Being earmarked in this way is not good for one's career in the caring professions – those who are deemed to have 'failed' often get overlooked for promotion, or at the very least, are not listened to. And yet, so-called 'failure' has at its root the seeds of change and development, if only we would learn to look at the root causes and see them as signposts for transformation.

Burn-out stalks those who care.

The concept of burn-out was first mooted in the 1970s by psychologists Christina Maslach and Susan Jackson. Herbert Freudenberger and colleague Gail North later went on to develop the Theory of Indicators for measuring the condition. According to Freudenberger and North, there are twelve recognisable stages of burn-out, which are not necessarily followed sequentially and you may not exhibit all of them, but if you feel you have one or more of these symptoms, it certainly is time to address the issues that have given rise to them.

1. The Compulsion to Prove Oneself
   This could be an overwhelming drive to succeed in the workplace or to feel excessive ambition. This is often expressed as determination and compulsion.

2. Working Harder
   The desire to prove yourself leads to high personal expectations at home and at work. This can lead to obsessive behaviour.

3. Neglecting Your Needs
   Being devoted to work or family in this way means that other things get neglected, such as your own needs and desires, even to the extent of neglecting to eat, sleep and take care of your appearance.

4. Displacement of Conflicts
   You may now be aware that something is not quite right, but you are unable to get to the

source of the problem. This is the point at which physical symptoms of dis-ease can be expressed, such as sleepless nights, anxiety, panic attacks etc.

5. Revision of Values
   In this stage, you may begin to isolate yourself from others, avoid potential conflicts, and fall into a state of denial towards your own basic physical needs. Your values may even start to change: because you have no energy left, you may become emotionally withdrawn and stop doing the things that once gave you pleasure.

6. Denial of Emerging Problems
   As time goes by, you may become intolerant of others, even to the point of being antisocial and aggressive. Other people will by now have noticed the change in you and may offer help and support but you will deny that there is anything wrong: "I'm okay – don't worry!"

7. Withdrawal
   Things can't go on like this and you may become withdrawn from family and friends and as a result turn to alcohol or drugs whether prescribed or not, to 'ease the pain.' Contact with others is now at a minimum, and could turn into isolation.

8. Obvious Behavioural Changes
   At this point, family, friends and other people in your immediate social circles will be aware

of the obvious changes in you and will try to intervene. They recognise the seriousness of the situation.

9. Depersonalisation

   You no longer feel valued and you lose track of your values and needs. Your view of life will have narrowed to the merely mechanical functions of 'keeping going.'

10. Inner Emptiness

    You feel an emptiness inside, and to overcome this, you might increase your intake of drugs, alcohol and other stimulants such as sex, to an unhealthy extent. You are looking to ease the pain in any way you can.

11. Depression

    Burn-out may, but not always, include depression. You are exhausted, you feel hopeless, indifferent, and believe that you have no future. Other typical depression symptoms may arise.

12. Burn-out Syndrome

    At this point, you may collapse physically and emotionally and should seek immediate medical attention. In extreme cases, usually only when depression is involved, suicidal thoughts may occur, which you may see as an escape from this dreadful situation. It is important to remember that very few people do actually commit suicide.

As you can see from these 12 Stages of Burn-out, this is a serious condition. Burn-out can lead to some very debilitating physical and mental symptoms, so don't ignore any of them. The important thing is to look at the root causes of these symptoms: what is at the root of your feeling this way? What can you do to change? Who can you turn to for help?

Change course and avoid the rocks!

Clearly, the thing to do here is change course and avoid the rocks! You have obviously recognised that something is wrong and that you are not happy with the way your life is progressing – this is a very good sign, as it means that you are still engaged enough with your own feelings and still care enough about yourself to change the direction that you are headed in, and although there may have been very low energy in your life for some time now, you are prepared to make the effort. Low energy and a feeling of emptiness are symptoms that are often labelled as depression; however I view these symptoms as precursors of change especially when coupled with a feeling that something should be happening, but without any clear idea what that might be. Something is brewing: it is a fomenting, fermenting and transformative time. The old you must die (figuratively speaking of course!) before the new you can be born.

This can be a hard time – transitions usually are – and you may want the change to happen instantly, but trust me, it won't. However, this 'waiting time' allows for a gradual metamorphosis into the new you (or the you that has simply been covered up). It can take time, it can be difficult and challenging, but we need to learn to honour these times in our lives, and remember that there are very few people, if any, who get through life without experiencing at least one episode that gets labelled (rightly or wrongly) as depression. As a society, we do not understand or appreciate the wisdom that, waiting patiently for the light to return, will bring. Sit tight and believe in the positive – I promise you that it is worth the wait. There will be laughter through the tears, and joy amidst the sorrow; you are a deep enough vessel to hold all of these things at the same time. Stop fighting yourself, let yourself be and begin the process of self-recognition. It is worth repeating that what we may see as symptoms of depression can actually be precursors of change, but for change to happen, something has to change! Your soul's inner whispers are attempting to reach you. Listen to them.

EXERCISE

Make sure you will be undisturbed and that that there will be no other calls on your time – do not rush this. Now make yourself comfortable, with your pen and your journal to hand. I would like you to reflect on burn-out. Answer these questions as honestly as you are able. Take your time and get to the heart of your answer. There may be more than one answer; you may assume more than one role. Note everything.

What role(s) do you assume that perpetuate the situations you no longer want in your life?

- Are you the Victim (I feel helpless and at the mercy of others)
- The Martyr (I help others in order to make myself feel better about me)
- The Vindicator (I turn on others for making me feel like this)
- The Instigator (I initiate a situation in order to create a role for myself)
- Other

Then ask yourself -

- Why were you drawn to this role?
- How long have you been doing this?
- Who taught you this role?
- What benefits do you gain from being in the situation(s)?
- Who are you trying to please and why?
- By assuming this role, what are you trying to avoid?
- What do you need to do to change this situation?
- What would be your future ideal scenario?
- How can you now begin steps towards this?

I have asked you to see new possibilities for your future, as these will act as an antidote to what you are currently experiencing, which can be termed 'the dark night of the soul'. In essence, this is the bleak wasteland that is the loss of contact with yourself.

> *It is imperative that you face your fear because ultimately, you are only facing yourself.*

It can be frightening to face your shadow (your caged tiger) because you don't know what will happen. Being afraid to cast a light on the caged tiger is part of the process of change, and the fear you may experience may have many aspects to it, but it is imperative that you face your fear because ultimately, you are only facing yourself – and you are not someone to be afraid of, are you?! Become yourself because there is nothing wrong with who you are. You are unique and amazing and there is only one of you. It is so important to remember that, as it can get lost in the confusion of your conflicting internal messages.

When you free your caged tiger and allow expression to all the pent-up emotions and energy that has been locked away, sometimes for years, it can be frightening for you and sometimes for the people around you. You were cut off from your essence and disconnected from your deeper feelings, from your creativity and the sense of meaning that makes life so worthwhile. No wonder you are exhausted or have felt that you are going mad. Even so, you must face the real you – including the fear that your loved ones may not like the changes in you. Painful as that might be, at least it means that you are actually not pretending to be someone else anymore.

Whenever you are feeling overwhelmed or out of control, stop whatever you are doing, make yourself comfortable and breathe deeply until you have created an inner stillness. There is nothing else to do except be supported by your breath. Let the space be inside you and breathe into it. Simply draw on your inner resources.

CHAPTER FOUR
STOP

"Give in to reality and accept it just as it is – then you give yourself the opportunity to change."
- IRENE BRANKIN

C hange is a scary prospect, but in our society the fear of change is generally far more debilitating than the actual process itself. The thing about change is that, as it happens regardless of your attitude to it, it is far better to be flexible enough to roll *with* the changes: if you can't do that change will roll over you and carry on regardless, leaving you floundering in its wake. A good example of that is the communications revolution. However you may feel about it, it appears to be here to stay! For those who have embraced it fully, technology is another useful tool that helps us to organise and structure our daily lives. This revolution has heralded seismic changes in the way we live and the way we think; it has enabled, facilitated and shaped our daily lives. You only have to watch an old movie ('Get Carter' springs to mind) to understand the vast differences in lifestyle that have taken place in just a generation or so. Communication is now instantaneous and taken for granted by almost everybody.

Consequently however, there is great deal of fear that has been generated by this wave of change: are our brains being fried by microwaves? How much danger are our children exposed to from easy access to dubious online content? How safe is our data? How safe is our privacy? How can we protect ourselves from unscrupulous online criminals? But in spite of all of this and more, it is extremely unlikely that things will go back to the way they were before the communications revolution. Those who live in fear of this change for whatever reason find themselves increasingly isolated on an island of technophobia. This inability or refusal to accept and deal with modern life as it is – whatever the reason – results in life becoming ever more bewildering and circuitous, as even the most mundane of tasks, like banking for example, have become fraught with difficulty, and therefore, reliance on the people who have embraced change becomes a daily occurrence.

I am not advocating that everyone should become a techno-wizard (and I am certainly not one of those!), I am just using this analogy to illustrate the kind of isolation and frustration that develops when we refuse to look at life as it really is, and what happens when we do not accept or compromise with the inevitability of change. If this denial is translated into our personal lives and into a refusal to look at what is really going on inside us, then we become detached from our own emotions. When we refuse to acknowledge our true feelings we make it impossible to introduce the possibility of change and we create our own island of isolation upon

which we build our tiger's cage. We are all changing
constantly, physically and emotionally throughout
the whole of our lives – we need change, however
painful and confusing it may be – because without
the vitality of change, there is only stagnation. To
personally initiate positive change in your own life
is one of the most empowering things you will ever
do. The more deeply grounded you are in your
actual reality, the more possibility exists for change.

Without the vitality of change, there is only stagnation.

So STOP, take stock of your life and get in touch
with yourself. Stopping in this respect does not
mean negating your everyday life, giving up or
falling into the stasis of depression – it means
STOP repeating the patterns that are making you
so unhappy, and do something about it. Such
change does not have to be sudden and drastic; you
do not have to completely reinvent yourself
overnight! Unless there is something dramatic
going on, change tends to happen in increments:
evolution itself takes time. Of course, you may feel
that it is time for something seismic to occur in
your life! If so, it is still a good idea to take the time
to think about and evaluate the truth of your life, to
come to terms with things as they actually are, to
put yourself fully in the picture. When you can
honestly assess the complexities and nuances of the
realities of your life, you will be able to begin the
process of change. The fact that you are reading

this book and are considering doing this is in itself a
harbinger of change. Do not be afraid of what is
inside you – of who you really are – and especially,
do not fear the part of you that is desperate for
change to happen. Listen to yourself because you
already know what you need.

EXERCISE

To facilitate this process and enable you to
understand the structures that have helped to create
your tiger's cage, I would like you to make a list of all
the things in your life that you consider you MUST
or SHOULD do. Everything you can think of
– large or small – that comes to mind can be included.
When you have done this I'd like you to analyse them.

- How many of the things on your list are
  actually motivated by some kind of fear? Fear
  can take many guises: fear of being judged;
  fear of being found wanting in some way; fear
  of failure or even of success!
- How much of what is on your list do you
  really care about?

How much of what you have listed is essential to
your life?

Now make a list of things you WANT TO do.
Include everything – the small things and the big
things and even the things you think are impossible.

- Is there anything on the MUST/SHOULD list that is also on the WANT TO list?
- What do you think this tells you?
- What is it that keeps you from fulfilling your potential to achieve what is on your WANT TO list?

Ultimately, it is only by focussing on your WANT TO list that you will fulfil your dreams and ambitions and in doing so, you will find out what your true 'needs' are, beneath the 'wants'.

We learn from our mistakes, but we are not doomed to repeat them.

You will succeed by listening to your own truths. If you take stock of what is happening in your life right now you will find that there is always a choice that you can make to change and enhance your life – it is never too late to change. If you continually look to the past for examples of failure then you will only succeed in convincing yourself that history is going to repeat itself. It is true that we learn from our mistakes, but we are not doomed to repeat them.

If it *is* the case that you have burnt-out and are trying to carry on as normal, please understand that there is nothing to be ashamed of in having to take time out. Indeed, anyone who has made a success of their life and career will readily admit that they have succeeded because of what 'failure' has taught them. Failure is painful to be sure, but it is a great teacher. It is rare for people to appreciate the courage that it takes to pick yourself up and start again when society in general rewards success and dismisses failure out of hand. No wonder your caged tiger has curled up in a ball in the corner of its cage and made itself as small as possible. There is no roar here! Yet everything you have experienced so far has brought you to this place and to this moment in time: this is the point at which you let go of the past and look towards the future; this is the point where you begin to give yourself the things that you need.

If you have been 'drowning not waving', this is the time to make a stand for your own potential. By taking stock in this way, you are waking up to your own responsibility in what has happened to your life: you are just as much a participant in your own burn-out as any other implicating factor; you have been in denial about your own reality and about the way you are living your life. It is time to regain your sanity and step away from the madness that you have allowed your life to become.

At this moment, you are aware of the effects of burn-out on your mind, body and spirit – but the difference is, you are taking steps towards recovery. The reality of your life is … that it is what it is. Now, what are you going to do to change or eradicate the things you don't want in your life anymore and create and initialise the things that you do?

EXERCISE

Sit comfortably with your spine straight. Uncross your arms and legs and loosen any tight clothing.

Begin to slow down your breathing and with each deep, slow breath, breathe in whatever it is you want to increase and have more of in your life and breathe out what you want to let go of.

Breathe in joy and breathe out stress

Breathe in light and breathe out darkness

Breathe in calm and breathe out anger …

You can imagine emotions as colours or you can simply breathe in for a count of four, hold it for four and exhale for a count of four.

NOW

TAKE A FRESH LOOK AT YOU – WHAT DO YOU SEE AND HEAR?

Take a little time and settle into yourself. Imagine that you're going to a celebration, a party in honour of you. It's a celebration of your life. As you walk in, look around and notice who is there. Look around – everyone is here to celebrate with you. Notice how they are towards you.

Now imagine that I walk in behind you and ask these people who know and care very much for you, "What is it you're celebrating about (your name)'s life? What are the qualities that you see in (your name) that she does not see in herself?

What have you heard about you as you take a fresh look at yourself?

Write it down.

Sometimes when we take stock of ourselves, we only look at what we have not achieved. I want you to list what you *have* achieved in the past and what you are working towards now. The achievements can be anything from the small to the large, for example: I worked hard and passed my 11+ or I know I looked great when I was at my son's wedding – to I became a Director of the organisation or I was a Trustee of a charity ... You can do this spontaneously or start from childhood and work up to where you are now; or you can work backwards from the present to childhood. Choose whatever suits you. Enjoy this process – take your time and really think about all the things you have achieved. I'm sure you will surprise yourself!

You can approach this in different ways: you can make it factual like a diary, with specific times and events noted, or write about how you were feeling about what was going on at the time, looking not just at your achievements but also taking note of your good qualities and attitudes. Take time to appreciate yourself.

This can take a while, but it is worth the effort as this is time spent on you: it is all about you. How often has that been the case in your life? By doing this exercise you are building up a picture of yourself – perhaps you have overlooked so much about you in the past? You are getting to know yourself again.

This exercise is all about being authentic; it is making a conscious choice to be real – to be honest and to allow your true self to be seen. This can be very difficult for us because as we expose our true selves, we make ourselves vulnerable. That is why most of us only manage to be authentic with certain people – exposing our true selves to our work colleagues or our family and friends may take us out of our comfort zones. Setting aside our need to be liked is frightening, and so mostly, we wear a mask. We mask our true selves to all but a very few.

We have all experienced at some point in our lives how cruel the world can be: we may have spoken honestly about an issue and had it taken out of context, creating a mountain out of a molehill. And so we retreat and put on our masks – once bitten, twice shy. There is a great fear of authenticity – of being ourselves – and a seemingly cohesive move to suppress it in society in general. Not only must we act a certain way as wives, mothers and lovers, but we must look a certain way too and like the same things culturally. To express our true selves, to be non-conformist, is seen to be odd and even dangerous! But just as dangerous is the festering resentment that is created by swallowing back anger and not expressing yourself honestly, which can lead to emotional and physical problems. Consistently suppressed anger does not miraculously dissipate; it tends to emerge in disguised ways. The consequences of social and family pressure to deny your true nature are manifold.

The exercise to look at yourself and your true nature is valuable, because it is important to risk expressing what you're not articulating in your life. If you don't do this, you are ultimately denying yourself the joy of authentic living. Focus on the WANT TO list (and the 'needs' that lie beneath them); focus on what you have achieved in your life; focus on who you want to be not who you feel you should be. Step over the threshold of your cage …

So, are you ready to wake-up to yourself and life? Are you prepared to re-connect with you, with all your gifts, abilities, skills and qualities? When you do this, you are recognising and acknowledging your true potential: you are taking steps towards a life where you can express your caring for yourself first, so that then, and only then, you can express your care for others. If you have ever been in an aeroplane watching the stewardess going through the safety procedures, you will have noticed that they stress that you put your own oxygen mask on first, before you put your child's oxygen mask on. This can seem harsh, as society has taught us to put others before ourselves, but if you do not give yourself the oxygen of life, you will have nothing to give others. This is an allegory worth remembering, because it is actually lifesaving.

Every time you exercise your right to say no, you are building up the muscle to say, "YES!"

You have to learn to say, "No" before you can move on. Again, every time you exercise your right to say no, you are building up the muscle to say, "YES!" with conviction. Saying, "I don't care ..." is hard, but in reality you are only saying, "I care about something else more," or "I am prioritising." As with learning to say no, when you allow your 'I don't care' muscle to express itself, you are stretching yourself and allowing yourself to exercise authority and choice, which in turn will enable you to see more clearly what it is that you do care about. If you love yourself first, everything in your life begins to fall into place.

By allowing 'I don't care' to have a voice, you may start to become aware that you're here for a higher purpose, even if you have no clear idea of what it is or how to go about it. Take stock of yourself first and you will have a better understanding of what is calling you to be visible in the world and this understanding will give you the courage to be your own unique self.

Who is that woman in the mirror? Do you know her? Do you see her as simply a wife, mother, businesswoman, grandmother, exercise-fanatic, dancer, a lady who lunches ... ? She may be all of those things, but does she have depth and substance, a rich inner-life? When we make no effort to escape the cage, we will stay in a rut, even if, on the surface, we are fulfilling a variety of roles. Ultimately, we have to look at who we are on the inside. Interestingly, the definition of a 'rut' is a shallow grave – this is a very good metaphor for the experience that so many of us go through at some point in our lives: burying ourselves in repetition and drudgery at the expense of our wellbeing and happiness. Staying in our well-defined rut and not facing our fear may seem easier and less threatening, but such inaction robs us of hope. If there is no hope, life can become unbearable.

The difference between caring for yourself and selfishness may not be immediately apparent, especially as our early conditioning has led us to believe that self-caring equates with selfishness, but self-caring it is exactly the opposite of selfishness – it is in fact the best thing you can do to ensure that you are able to help others (remember the aeroplane oxygen analogy). If you are not adequately nourished, it is all but impossible to adequately nourish others. When you make space for yourself, you will re-connect with what's important to you. You will be ready to acknowledge the woman you used to be and incorporate her and the dreams and possibilities she represents into the woman you are, and the woman you want to become.

It is never too late to do what you want to do in whatever way you want to do it.

When you allow yourself freedom of expression – the freedom not to care and the freedom to say no – you will begin to be able to breathe more easily, and because you can breathe more easily, you will have more energy. More energy brings renewed hope and you will start to see all the things in your life that you can be grateful for. The narrow confines of your cage will become ever more clear and ever more unsustainable. You will finally be able to acknowledge that the tiger wants OUT: that it is time to stop being a people pleaser and allow that "No!" to surface. You do not have to be a 'Yes' woman (as that in itself brings untold difficulties), but you can be yourself. You don't have to have the approval of others or hide behind a façade of niceness. You now know how to stop being manipulated by the world; there is no law that says you have to be who anyone else wants you to be! Isn't that amazing – you can be you! It is now time to become aligned with yourself. You have come through burn-out and listened to your inner-self. It is a revelation to many women that I have worked with that it is never too late to do what you want to do in whatever way you want to do it. You owe yourself the opportunity to come back to yourself.

A measure of selfishness is healthy! Yes really, despite the years of being told the complete opposite, caring for yourself is effectively a matter of holding positive attitudes towards yourself without feeling guilty about it. Sometimes it is necessary to be 'self-ish' in the sense of balancing your own needs with those of others in order not to be put upon. The benefits of setting boundaries are immense, because it says to the world, "I'm a person in my own right". This is basic self-respect and wanting things for yourself does not negate your true caring for others. Taking your own needs into account is simply a way to include yourself in the picture. Now is the time to begin!

For change to happen, change has to happen.

Change almost always encounters resistance: the changes you are about to make in your life are likely to encounter resistance from some of the people you know who are quite happy with the way they perceive you. But if they truly care for you, then they will want what is best for you too. Some of the people and situations that are part of your life now may have to drop away as the real you emerges. This may be difficult and even painful but you now know what happens when you keep your tiger locked up. For change to happen, change has to happen. You have felt the energy contained within; you know that it is a dangerous and destructive energy, so powerful that it could kill; an energy so completely turned in on itself that it has almost killed you. Now it's time to let that energy out, to make changes and to release the roar of the tiger.

Caring for yourself is effectively a matter of holding positive attitudes towards yourself without feeling guilty about it!

In conclusion then, it *is* possible to take life seriously and yet live lightly and joyfully. It doesn't matter if your friends and family find the changes you are making challenging. You have to be authentic to the deep 'you' inside: other people are not you, only you are you. Life is a learning process, it is both dark and light and without the darkness we would never understand what it means to come into the blessedness of the light. One cannot exist without the other, no matter how much we wish it were otherwise. To care for yourself is to make a conscious choice to move into the light, and walk the line of balance and harmony in your life. This is your first step out of the tiger's cage and it may feel like a tightrope walk, but with practice, you will get good at it!

VISUALISATION EXERCISE

The following exercise is a cathartic experience learned in psychosynthesis training. It is powerful and you do need to be 'held' in a safe place inside or outside, where no one can hear you! It is highly recommended to have someone with you that you completely trust – a friend, or a psychosynthesis practitioner, who can guide you through the visualisation exercise below. By guiding, I mean to calmly lead you through the steps, in sequence, reading the visualisation to you as you enact it. The reader should give you time to absorb and visualise each step before proceeding to the next. If this is not an option then I suggest that you acquaint yourself thoroughly with the exercise before you attempt it, or download the exercises as audio files using this link – http://www.thevisiblewoman.com/ recordings – where I will take you through each exercise step by step.

I would like you to stand up, close your eyes and take three deep breaths – in for four, hold for four, out for four – allowing yourself to get in touch with your caged tiger. Reach down to the place inside you where the cage constrains the tiger. See the cage: what does it look like, what it is made of? Visualise your tiger trapped behind the bars, feel the prowling presence of your tiger, see the glow behind the eyes, feel the restless pent up fury.

You have a key in your hand – how big is it, how heavy, what is it made of? Now unlock the door and step inside the cage, leaving the door swinging open. Move toward the tiger, allowing the energy of the tiger to permeate your being and as you slowly approach nearer and nearer your own energies are merging with your tiger. Reach out and touch your tiger – do not be afraid of your inner self – and as your hand touches the tiger, you become a part of each other: you absorb each other – you and the tiger are becoming one: you are the tiger, and the tiger is you.

Pace up and down inside that cage and really feel the energy, the passion and anger. Allow this energy to rise up through your body: feel the rage and frustration rising up through your stomach and now your chest and up into your throat. Allow what happens to happen. Do not block any of the emotions – allow any sounds or noises to come out, with no judgement or censoring.

As you allow the sounds and noises and feelings to emerge from your being, you may find they are accompanied by movements – you might even want to pound a cushion or push against something! Give yourself permission to go with whatever has been locked away for too long. Get in touch with the underlying cause of the feelings you are expressing.

This is the roar of your caged tiger.

You may find that there are also tears from locked-away grief and sorrow that has been stored up since childhood and added to as you've gone through life. This is why you have been so afraid of it letting it out, afraid that the destruction it can cause will be too great. But do not be afraid – trust the process and let it out.

When you feel you have completed this exercise, take time to write about it in detail: the images that came up, the events, the people, and how you feel about what just happened. If it has gone according to plan, you will have just released years of anger and pain suppressed by years of conditioning. As a good, caring person, concerned with being seen as 'nice and respectable', you were unable to let it out for fear of criticism, censure, guilt and shame. Do not feel afraid, do not feel guilt, do not feel shame – instead allow that incredible energy to release and feel the freedom that it brings in its stead.

I have experienced the cathartic release of this exercise. When I allowed this to happen, I felt liberated and joyful, as if a physical weight had been lifted from my body. I expressed the nature of my anger. I released my caged tiger. I became lighter and energised, and far more myself. And this is what I want for you.

CHAPTER FIVE
CARE LESS

Selfish = self-ish = taking care of self

Most of us tend to equate caring less with a hardening of the heart. How many times have you heard or used the expression, "I couldn't care less" to convey a contemptuous dismissal of someone or something that has the potential to hurt? This is the opposite of what this chapter is all about; we do not need to discover new ways in which to shellac our feelings – the smothering of our true self is what has contributed to the frustration and imprisoning of your tiger in the first place. This chapter is an exploration of a way of thinking and of interacting with ourselves and the people in our lives which encourages and enables us to dismantle the constructs that society and our culture has forged around us – ie: our cage. This passive acceptance of the unspoken rules and limitations that have hitherto governed our behaviour and responses are no longer acceptable to us – it is time to care less!

To care less does not have to mean that you give less care or you are careless. It can and will mean that you free yourself up and are able to care more for what is important to you. The more you can express true caring that comes from the heart, the more it will impact positively, not only in your own life but in the lives of those around you. Like a pebble thrown into a pond, the ripples that spread outward from the centre of true care will continue to widen, expand and touch others. The integrity of action that springs from genuine caring is far more likely to enrich your soul and bring true joy into your life and the lives of those you love than the deadening exhaustion that is engendered by fighting your honest inclinations.

Give yourself the consideration and respect that you have been giving others.

I want you to find your true voice, so that when you express yourself from a place of care-less-ness those who have ears to hear you will then have an example of how to be. You will become a role model – and in this day and age of youth culture, obsession with body image and shallow materialism, positive role models for women are desperately needed. Once you have an awareness of yourself and start to understand and evaluate your experiences then you can begin to live more lightly in body and mind. Once you start to act consciously – to do something to change your life – to care less – the weight and oppression of hypocrisy will begin to fall away.

This is where you begin to behave as an adult and have a say in your life. You're no longer that child;

you are all grown up and can take care of yourself and your child within. So start treating yourself fairly, give yourself the consideration, respect and space that you have been giving others. Start to like yourself – why not! You have painted yourself into a corner on behalf of other people; you have been more than you needed to be, more than was good for you. You are a decent human being so forgive yourself for your past and start liking the woman you are becoming. You don't have to be perfect or live up to other people's – or even your own – expectations; you don't have to be a good person according to anyone else's definition. You just have to like yourself – how hard is that? If you love and respect yourself others can follow suit.

EXERCISE

Take a deep breath to centre yourself. Breathe in for a count of four, hold for a count of four and breathe out for a count of four.

Now do the same breathing again and as you breathe in tell yourself

> *"I don't have to be perfect."*

As you hold the breath tell yourself

> *"I have nothing to prove."*

As you breathe out tell yourself

"I like who I am."

Do this three times and then, on the fourth breath, try out

"I love me"

When you breathe into those words, it can help you gain perspective on life and improve your self-respect. Self-respect is important; it is a factor that determines not only how you feel about yourself, but how other people perceive you. It is important to remember that self-deprecation (condemnation or disapproval) is not the same thing as humility. True modesty is not a mechanism for the belittling of who you are or of your achievements. Self-respect is encouraged by acknowledging yourself, by tuning-in to your honest response to a request or situation. If your response is, "I don't want to be part of this", then listen to that. "I don't want to be a part of this" is not the same thing as, "I wish I wasn't a part of this". You have a choice: if you don't want to be part of something, don't be – but don't just waste your life wishing you were doing something else. What is helpful to understand in yourself is how much you really care about the situation that you are presented with: is the outcome important to you? Do you really care or are you just responding in the way you have led yourself and others to expect?

As we have discussed in previous chapters, we are taught to be compliant from a very early age. The ability to refuse – to not give more than you care to – is not something that can just be switched on, it has to be practised. 'No' is a word that has negative connotations. We reach out for something shiny when we are babies and hear, "No!" We want a toy another child is playing with and we are told, "No!" We want another ice cream we are told, "No!" and so it goes on. The word 'No' becomes seriously negative in our lives and yet when we as children start to exercise the power of 'No' it does not work for us – it appears to infuriate and enrage: "Don't you say no to me!" is a common response of a parent to a defiant child. So we learn that to say 'No' becomes the prerogative of others.

You can start right now practising your 'No'. Remember the last situation in which you said yes to something that you really did not want to do? What would have happened if you had said no? Would the world have stopped spinning on its axis? Would a bolt of lightning have struck you down? I suspect not! Things might have been a bit awkward for a minute or two and then life would have carried on. It is not a crime to say no. Saying no is not about looking after number one and being arrogant, it's about knowing that you are worthy of love, from yourself and from others. This understanding will make you a happier person and if you are happier then your home is happier. The 'JUST SAY NO' advertising campaign of the 1990's was aimed at young people to help them deal with the pressures involved in the drug culture. I am invoking that spirit now! If you really do not want to do it, JUST SAY NO.

When you say no to doing something for others (or whatever it is that you are asked to do but don't want to do) this doesn't mean you don't care. It means that you are including yourself in the equation; it does not mean that you are a bad and selfish person. There is a choice and it is yours to make so listen to yourself and decide what feels right, even if that appears to go against what is perceived as socially acceptable. The next time you feel you are being emotionally blackmailed into participating in something that you really don't care about, try saying no very quickly. If you find later in the conversation that you do want to participate, you can always be magnanimous and change your mind. You will have exercised your choice instead of automatically falling-in with someone else's needs. Listen to yourself and learn to trust your inner voice.

There is a choice and it is yours to make so listen to yourself and decide what feels right.

Here are some suggestions of how to present your "No" that will enable you to create boundaries and establish your autonomy. The aim here is to learn to say no without apology.

- Say, "No, I can't today." This implies that you are busy, you also have a life and you do not have to explain yourself. Above all, you do NOT have to feel guilty if the other person has a problem with your refusal.
- Broken Record – this is the repetition of your assertive refusal each time: "No, I can't today." You wear the other's resistance down with sheer repetition.
- Reflecting – reflecting back the content and feeling of the request and adding your assertive refusal, e.g. "I know you've got to finish it, even so, I can't help you today".
- Reasoned No – gives very briefly the genuine reason for the no, e.g. "I can't help you because I have to…"
- Take a raincheck - saying no to the present request but leaving room for negotiation for a future yes.
- Clarification – this isn't a definite 'No' and can be a prelude to negotiation as it asks for further information e.g. "Can you start any of it today without me?"
- Simply No – say, "No" and nothing else.

You may find that other people resist your 'No' by being hostile. They may try to hurt you with sarcasm, abuse you verbally and express their perception of you as unreasonable, questioning what you say in order to confuse or distract you from your decision. Some may even try the emotional blackmail of pathos, complete with tears and pleading. This is very hard to resist, but resist you must, for your own sake. Some people may emotionally or physically withdraw by refusing to respond to you and actually walk away from you. Although people may retaliate, they are usually limited by the same conditioning that has kept you down! When you breathe into the place of 'care less' and tell yourself "I am on *my* side now" and stand firm and support yourself, you will find that it isn't as bad as you thought it would be. And although confrontation can be distressing, ask yourself this: "If this person is reacting to my perfectly reasonable need to have a life of my own and resents my choice to decide how best to expend my energy, how much does this person care about me?"

THE ART OF DIVINE INDIFFERENCE

If the choices that the new and assertive you make, means that some people no longer understand who you are, that is not your problem – it is theirs! When you are comfortable in your own shoes, you will have no need to justify and defend your decisions. You are fine just as you are and when you believe this yourself, simply being who you are will draw those to you who are attracted to and influenced by your truth and integrity. This 'Divine Indifference' is about being fearless in your endeavours to be true to yourself

even if it means that you risk rejection. It is not
about not caring!

None of this is easy and the transformation is going
to take time, but practice is the key. Start today: say
no to the next thing that does not warrant the
expenditure of your energy and keep on doing it
until eventually you find that you have grown up
and are standing firm in your own shoes. Instead of
worrying what others think – focus on what *you*
think and how *you* can express yourself in the
world. Don't apologise for being yourself. Some will
like you and some won't.

*'Divine Indifference' is about being fearless in your
endeavours to be true to yourself.*

There is nothing to be ashamed of in coming from
a position of caring less, in fact the very opposite is
true: you can be proud of the fact that you have
discovered your own values. Of course, it is
wonderful to be part of our families' and friends'
support networks and to be able to contribute to the
nurturing of others (both personally and
professionally) in their attempt to be the best that
they can be; it is rewarding and uplifting to watch
our children and our grandchildren flourish – but
apart from when children are very young, I do not
believe that we were put on this earth to sacrifice
ourselves on the altar of everybody else's wants and
needs. You have every right to take care of your

own needs too. Getting into the habit of unnecessarily putting others first, means that you will not grow into who you really are.

We were not put on this earth to sacrifice ourselves on the altar of everybody else's wants and needs.

The case study below is an example of one woman's realisation that she could care less and so free herself from the guilt and fear that a lifetime of self-sacrifice had engendered. The understanding that all her guilt and anguish merely added to the sum total of the same led her to the profound realisation that by adopting a 'care less' attitude, her life and the lives of those around her could actually be improved.

THE DAY I DECIDED TO PUT MYSELF FIRST

"I have brought up three children single-handedly. During their childhood I have been their mother, teacher and even their doctor as I decided years ago to protect them from the ravages of mainstream Western medicine.

Due to irreconcilable differences exacerbated by my husband's drinking, I ended up being the sole provider for my family as their father conveniently forgot that he had anything to do with bringing them into this world!

Of course, there were years of childcare, and along with the joys and rewards there were times when it was fraught with difficulty. It is hard enough when there are two parents but being alone with the responsibility meant that there were times of enormous stress and hardship ... and then one day, inevitably, they all leave ... and I'm alone.

This led to the big question typical of the empty nest syndrome: what am I going to do with the rest of my life? Suddenly I had no immediate responsibilities except to myself. This is recognised as a difficult time for many women and for a woman who has had no partner with whom to plan for a child-free future, it can be a very bleak time indeed.

Worse still is when it seems that all your hard work has been in vain, as happened to me one day during an argument with one of my children, where I was criticised and savaged for all the 'mistakes' I made as a parent. I retaliated by saying that my efforts had been a damn sight better than anything their other conspicuously absent parent had ever done, only to be told that I had nothing to be proud of as I'd only acted as any parent should. Which of course is true, but this appraisal of my shortcomings gave me no credit for the years of self-sacrifice and showed no appreciation of my situation let lone any acknowledgement of the difficulties and terrors of lone-parenting.

Apparently I had done everything wrong: I had been a BAD mother. All that effort for all those years had been pointless and thankless. I was a worthless parent and a failed wife. I had no future and less hope. I quickly slipped into an abyss of depression and self-loathing, convinced I was a total failure.

But the human spirit is a remarkable thing and somehow I would not let myself give up on me, so I invested in myself for the first time in my life and I sought help. The sessions that I attended had an accumulative effect – no earth-shattering realisations or blinding revelations, but I gradually gained perspective and a renewed sense of optimism, and eventually I 'saw the light' and realised how futile all my guilt and sadness was. What exactly was I achieving by constantly beating myself up about the past? I had done my best but apparently it wasn't good enough and maybe in at least one person's eyes it never would be.

I decided to stop caring about whether I had been a good mother or not, or whether I had been a good *anything* or not. It was all in the past anyway and apart from making an effort to understand it, there was nothing I could do about it – but I had the rest of my life in front of me. I decided to forgive myself for my mistakes – both real and imagined – and move on. One day my children will be parents themselves and then they will be in a position to appreciate what I did for them … or maybe they

never will appreciate it. Either way, it
doesn't matter!

These days I don't care what my kids think: I have
done my best and that is all anyone can do – neither
do I care what the world thinks. I may not have
gotten it right, but at least I tried! My children have
survived and have the freedom to say what they
think, and their intelligence has been nurtured at
least enough for them to be able criticise their
upbringing. Whatever I may or may not have
achieved in their eyes, they are all still here to
berate me with my failings! I have come to realise
that my role as a mother is just that: a role – it does
not define *me* – it is just one role of many I will play
in this life. This does not mean that I do not care
about my children and it does not mean that I do
not love them; it means that I now know what is
important both to me and for me and am not
bogged down in other people's expectations of what
I should have been or what I ought to be.

These realisations have freed me to explore all the
other aspects of myself, and share my
understanding and knowledge with the world
around me.

What luxury! What freedom!"

EXERCISE

THE MEADOW OF LIMITLESS POSSIBILITY

After reading the courageous sharing of the above case study, I would like you to ready yourself for the next exercise which will help you to tap into the source of creativity within you.

Take a deep breath: in for a count of four, hold for four and out for four. Do this three times – this will help you focus and turn your attention inwards.

I want you to consider where in your body you feel your wisdom resides and breathe into this part of your body. As you breathe in, let the breath infuse this part of yourself with light.

Now imagine you are standing in a meadow – this is the meadow of limitless possibility. However you see the meadow is fine – don't worry about how you imagine the meadow to be: do not judge or censor the image. As you look out over your meadow you can see that it is surrounded by fields: each of these fields represents limitless support for the realisation of your hopes and aspirations.

As you stand in the meadow of limitless possibility surrounded by support, ask yourself these questions:

- What do I most deeply desire to experience in my life?
- What do I most wish to express through living my life?
- What do I want to create in my life?
- What do I most desire to contribute to others and the world?

Simply be open to receiving, and welcome in any awareness you have of the answers, which may come in words or symbols or images – stay open and be welcoming to whatever you receive.

When you are ready, take a final look around your meadow then take your leave of this place and make your way back to the world.

Write in your journal everything that you can recall of the experience. You may find that answers will come later in unexpected and synchronistic ways: through something someone says or through something you read, or through the lyrics in a song. Be open to these possibilities and do not dismiss them as coincidence or happenstance.

Finally I suggest that you begin to put into action any answers that have come to you.

Your life force demands expression; when you wake up to your potential and discover the ability to focus on your own needs and fulfilment, you rediscover the magic in your life. When you care less about the world's perception of you, your ability to give the things you do care about your best shot will be amplified, as you are no longer squandering your energies.

"Death is not the biggest fear we have: our biggest fear is taking the risk to be alive – the risk to be alive and express who we really are."
– DON MIGUEL RUIZ

For example, when I was doing my first degree (BSc [Hons] Psychology) this was something I felt had to do to prove to the world: that I had intelligence and could have gone to university when I was younger. I put myself under immense pressure merely to conform to a standard and an expectation that I felt compelled to respond to. I did not study the subject purely for its own sake and as a result, although I achieved my aim, I became seriously exhausted and depleted. My second degree (MSc in Counselling Psychology) I undertook for myself. I wanted to learn and was immersed and interested. Of course, I was still under pressure, but it was pressure I chose to put myself under in order to gain knowledge of something fascinating. This time it was on my own terms and for myself. I was careless of what others thought; I was not trying to be accepted, I was not fighting my true inclinations and my ego was not in charge. It was my choice pure and simple. I was being who I was meant to be – expressing myself. As a result, although I was at times pretty mentally exhausted by my studies, I was not depleted in the same way as I was studying for my first degree. I was in fact energised and excited by my understanding of my chosen field.

Having fun is just as important in your adult life as it was when you were a child.

True self-expression is spontaneous – it is okay to have a crazy side! I am not talking psychosis here: if the voices are telling you to murder the dog its probably best if you keep on taking the tablets! The craziness I am referring to is the part of you that knows how to play – that treats life lightly. When you are rigid and locked in on yourself you are excluding joy. Remember when you were young? Your imagination was limitless – all the things you could be and do with just a cardboard box and a bedsheet. What fun it was, and even more so when others joined in. Remember how it felt to just get lost in play? As an adult you still need to play – the games might be different but having fun is just as important in your adult life as it was when you were a child.

Take some time to think about that: how would you like to play? Maybe a salsa or tango class? Maybe a dramatic society or a choir? Maybe a painting class? What would best express the creative aspect of your personality? You deserve to make this space for yourself – it will help you to open your heart and express the unique gifts that you have kept under wraps for too long. Do not neglect yourself for even one more day! The best investment you will ever make is in yourself because there is only one of you and you owe it to yourself to be the best 'You' possible.

You know it makes sense! Let yourself out, let yourself breathe … Learn to say "No!" to pointless energy expenditure and "Yes!" to your dreams.

CHAPTER SIX
CARE FREE

Come to the edge, Life said.
They said: We are afraid.
Come to the edge, Life said.
They came.
Life pushed them,
And they flew.
- GUILLIAME APPOLLINAIRE

Liberation! What does this word conjure up for you? In any language it represents freedom from oppression. This is what you are longing for – you want your freedom – and with the tiger roaring encouragingly in your ears, you are now working towards your own liberation. You have realised that the only person who can release you from the chains of mindless resignation is … yourself! Now is the time to break the bonds of slavery to convention and expectation, in order to creatively expand into the space that becomes available when you no longer force yourself to spend your time and energy conforming to ideas and ideals that actually have no real meaning for you. To have recognised your needs and undertaken this journey is astoundingly brave, so take some time to look back and see how far you have come.

Freeing your tiger is the single most vital process in living the rest of your life as a conscious human being.

Freeing the tiger, energising and liberating as it is, will not however be your passport to spending the rest of your life in the Elysian Fields! Unfortunately, it will not solve all your problems in one fell swoop, nor will it guarantee you an easy life. But, it is the single most vital process in living the rest of your life as a conscious human being. It is the focus of radical change within you that will release untold new energy, and this energy will go a long way towards helping you to cope with life in all its beauty and pain, both good and bad. When you are no longer being eaten up by unspoken resentments and exhausted by pointless activities, your emotional, mental and physical health will improve, your focus will be sharper and without all the unnecessary baggage, your life will be simpler and very much lighter

I want to emphasise that being carefree is not a selfish thing – having read this book, you know by now that a sense of caring should come from the heart and not from duty. Being carefree is about relinquishing that binding sense of duty so that you can embrace the world from the heart. Along with joy, the ability to truly care will undoubtedly bring you pain, but when you commit your energies to that which really matters to you, your caring will not be accompanied by a sinking of the heart and a diminishing of the spirit. This does not mean that it will be easy: sometimes committing to the things you truly care about may be extraordinarily difficult and even heartbreaking. You may have to brace yourself to take on the pain of another or find the inner strength to stand up to a situation or way of life which has kept you silent for years. Facing life head on takes courage. It is a painful process to confront your reality, to open your eyes to the facts of your life and no longer allow yourself to sleepwalk through life sedated by your drugs of choice, be they food, TV, work, alcohol, sex or whatever. It is not an easy journey at all. But once you begin, you have to go on – there is no going back and believe me it is worth the effort.

Carrying the weight of the world on your shoulders is only going to break your back.

Because of our conditioning we have a default mechanism that is set to 'Worry & Guilt'. Say "No" and we automatically feel bad about it! Worry and guilt kick-in and merely serve to undermine and deplete our inner resources. I am not talking about conscience or remorse here – these are different emotions that allow us to look more deeply at our actions and reactions and both of which are usually the precursors to an act of contrition or atonement. No, guilt and worry are quite different. Guilt is a pernicious vampire and worry is the enemy of action. Of course, I understand that worry is something that we all experience to varying degrees, but worry expended on situations over which we have no control and can effect no change will quickly become anxiety. So my advice here is this: If there is something you can do, do it – if there is nothing you can do, stop worrying! Easier said than done, but it is possible. I want you to think back to the last time that guilt or worry led to any effectual resolution in your life. Carrying the weight of the world on your shoulders is only going to break your back. So, decide what is truly yours, what really matters to you, and ditch the rest. You *can* do that: all you have to do is allow yourself to do it!

Next time you find yourself heading down 'Worry & Guilt' road it is a helpful support mechanism to say "I Don't Care!" to yourself a few times. You'll end up laughing – well smiling at least! This will help you to not get so bogged-down again. Remember, you are your own person.

EXERCISE

This gives you an opportunity to map out your best-case scenario – your next step. So take your time and relax. Don't rush this as it is important.

Get your journal and find a quiet place where you will not be disturbed. Take some deep breaths: in for four … and out for four … Do this until you feel you have centred yourself and cleared your mind.

Now do your best to clearly and coherently outline what you believe your next step should be. By 'next step' I mean whatever process or action you think needs to occur in your life to help you to progress. Only you will know what this is. It can be anything: whatever it is that *you* need, from "I need to be more confident," to "I want to change my job".

Once you've identified and outlined your next step, imagine yourself seated at a round table with five people that you most admire (alive or dead) and for whom you have great respect. Ask each of them, "What do I have to do to realise my best case scenario?" Stay open to receiving the answers in *whatever* form they come and write them down.

When all have responded, enjoy and appreciate the answers you have received, as you have been assessed by the best in yourself.

Be The Change – it starts with us!

The important message here is that being open to taking care of yourself *first* brings about change in the world. But it starts with us! As you begin to bring your aspirations to life, ask yourself to identify three simple things you can do this week towards your goal, then take the easiest step first. The more you make the changes you need, the easier it will get and the stronger you will become. Be aware that others are likely to dig their heels in and resist these changes in you as it affects their world, so choose your friends wisely at this delicate time of new beginnings. That which is new and tender is vulnerable and easily crushed, so do not expose yourself to those who are unlikely to understand. If you start to feel overwhelmed by the less than enthusiastic responses of others, breathe into that place inside you that knows you are doing the right thing *for you*. Tell yourself "I deserve whatever I need to bring about this change". Rest assured that if you look after yourself, then others will benefit.

> *'Be there for others but never leave yourself behind'*
> – DODINSKY

All of us have the right to feel valued. When we are unappreciated or taken for granted, resentment and tension are the results. In worse case scenarios, we begin to believe that we are worthless, but when we are sure of our own value, these petty intrusions into our sense of self are like water off of a duck's back. The shortsighted selfishness of others simply ceases to impact in the same way and as a result, our attitude and therefore our entire lives are lighter. When you value yourself you are far more able to value others and the world, and as a by-product other people will feel good in the presence of someone who is 'on purpose'. By this I mean that by living with awareness, you are bringing a sense of purpose into your daily life and you will find that when you operate out of this place with generosity of spirit, you are enhanced both spiritually and emotionally and others will respond to you in a far more positive way.

Life is full of paradox!

Obviously, there will be many situations and people that you still care about very much and in the newness of your cathartic "I Don't Care!" you may find that the creative tension of holding opposites – I don't care and I do care – can be difficult at first, but this is one of life's great truths and it enables you to comprehend the bigger picture. Life is full of paradox: it is quite possible to be a caring person whilst not caring about a great many things! It is even possible to decide to care about something when you have the time and energy to do so, but maybe not today. This does not make you a bad person; it makes you a rational one. In the words of F. Scott Fitzgerald, "The test of a first-rate intelligence is the ability to hold two opposing ideas in the mind at the same time, and still be able to function". Or as Roberto Assagioli says, "It is about Both – And".

Deciding how, where and when to best expend your energies is the mark of a person who knows, understands and accepts themselves. Over-commitment is not a good thing, as nothing and no one gets the right kind of attention from someone who is always fretting about the rest of the 'stuff on the list'. Sometimes life gets hectic, the unexpected happens and we have to pull out all the stops, but this kind of frenetic living should be the exception not the rule, unless of course you actually like it that way!

If you are unhappy about the way your time is being used, *now* is always the time to change things. When you can handle your life creatively yet lightly, you are aligned with yourself. To keep it simple, to be able to be frivolous as well as serious – that's what it's all about. Then you will be able to keep your balance even through the dark times.

Imagine you are working in a garden: you will see that some plants need a lot of attention, pruning, watering, weeding, etc. Others are hardier and need less care, but for the garden to thrive regular and concerted effort is required. The ground needs to be prepared and the right tools are essential and even when the garden is doing well, routine maintenance is what keeps you on top of it. Obviously this is a rather simplistic analogy, but there is still something to be said for it as like that garden, some aspects of your personality will need nurturing and protection some will need weeding out, you may have to prune and train, but most of all you just need to be well watered and bask in the sunshine!

"There is no passion to be found in settling for a life that is less than the one you are capable of living."
– NELSON MANDELA

Once you have ascertained what is really important to you – what you are willing to expend your energies on and what you are most definitely jettisoning – you will be exercising freedom of choice, and the more choices you exercise the stronger your 'Ability to Choose' muscle becomes. Sometimes your choices will be relatively simple, and at other times a little more complicated. The art of diplomacy will definitely come in handy, and you will become a dab-hand at knowing who or what you want in your life and who or what you most definitely do not. It all comes down to what you are willing to do and what you are not willing to do – it really is that simple. Being willing to do something is not at all the same thing as feeling that you *ought* do it and although of course we all have to compromise sometimes, life is not all about compromise and especially, it is not about you always being the one to make the compromise.

Stand tall and be proud of yourself: you are a woman in your own right, who has the roar of the tiger at her disposal and can make more choices than ever before. You are unique; there is no one else like you. Where you have come from and the journey you have been on in order to get to where you are now is your story, it belongs to no one else.

This is your reality; you are your own inspiration for change.

EXERCISE

Close your eyes and focus on your breathing in order to centre yourself. Take a couple of deep breaths and on the third in-breath feel love filling your heart as you breathe deeply into the words, "I am (your name) and I am unique. There is nobody else who is able to offer the world what I have to offer." As you exhale breathe-out any stress that you are holding in any part of your body. Do this exercise for five repetitions.

In this exercise you are concentrating on receiving. When you are able to receive from yourself then you are ready to receive from others. Be grateful for your life and live it in complete trust of your uniqueness. You deserve to give and equally you deserve receive. Connect with yourself.

"Whatever you can do, or dream you can do, begin it: boldness has genius, power and magic in it."
– GOETHE

So … as a woman in her own right, exercising free will and open to new experiences you can now say, "Yes!" to invitations and opportunities. You can say yes in this way, with enthusiasm and passion because you are able to say no to all those things that have previously bound you to convention and tied you up in knots of guilt and worry. "No" to all that, and "Yes!" to new experiences, because who knows what might happen? Who you will meet? Or what you will learn? Be curious and open to having fun. Don't withhold your enthusiasm for life, instead allow your childlike enjoyment to surface: no holding back – go for it! Remember to be a life-long learner at anything and everything. True motivation has to come from within so no more suppression and denial of the joy of authentic living.

You will no longer have to fear the disapproval of others because you don't really care about what they think. You have confidence in yourself and your decisions – so you can dismiss uncalled for comments and trust yourself. You will be stronger simply because you are stepping into and are comfortable in your own shoes rather than hobbled and impeded by the bad fit of those whose footsteps you have previously been following.

Those around you will know that you really mean your yes or no and will respect and trust you for it. Instead of worrying what others think, you can now focus on how you can express yourself in the world. Because you have stopped caring so much, you will stop trying to be accepted. You will become more comfortable within yourself and accept that some will like you, and some will not. Your legacy is about taking risks, being brave and not about others liking you. You do care, but about people and things that make a difference.

Acceptance of yourself with all your strengths and weaknesses is no guarantee that you will never again be caught up in the turmoil of emotional bad weather, but it will enable you to be real, to be yourself and to acknowledge and understand what is going on inside you. You will be clearer and more analytical of your processes, which enables a far greater likelihood of making the right decisions. Once you start to recognise certain aspects of your nature and question your own motivations rather than merely reacting, you begin to live a conscious life.

Of course you will still be human, so you might do things outside your boundaries in order to play the game or you might toy with people and events you're not really interested in – that's your choice! The difference is that you will have an awareness of what you are doing and you will not be measuring your behaviour against a standard that others have created. Should you fall short or exceed, it will be in your opinion and by your standards. This might make things confusing sometimes, as you will in effect be rewriting your rulebook, but it is infinitely preferable to merely responding to automatic programming. Whenever I see my grandchildren dancing to their own tune it reminds me to do the same. We do not have to corset ourselves into a shape that distorts our nature, we can take the damn thing off and breathe freely!

None of us are here forever, so recognise your own mortality. Life is short and this is a wake-up call not to spend your life fretting over what people may think – not to waste your precious time on things that are irrelevant or meaningless, because this is the epitome of futility. In a hundred years there will be very little, if any trace of your passage through this world – how often do you ever contemplate the life and times of your own great grandmother? Who will remember how you spent your life? Who will even care? In this, your one, precious lifetime, practising Divine Indifference is the key to opening the tiger's cage and is also the Rosetta Stone to understanding your true nature.

So celebrate your life! You are here, you are resilient and you are fully alive! Enjoy yourself: get up on that dance floor and do your own thing, make a fool of yourself, sing along to the radio at the top of your voice! To hell with what others may think, because that is *their* problem. How many people do you know who have to be absolutely plastered before they can dance or sing or express any spontaneous joy? This is a great tragedy – no one should have to poison themselves before they are able to express a spontaneous joyful impulse! There is something wrong in a culture of repression and whilst by some standards we live in a very free society indeed, emotionally many of us still have a long way to go before we attain the kind of liberation we have been working towards in this book. Remember, Divine Indifference is about being fearless, to risk rejection and be true to yourself.

Whatever it is that you want to do in your life, begin today.

Take heart, shine the light and have courage. You may make mistakes along the way, but that is how we learn – perhaps the only way we learn. Whatever it is that you want to do in your life, begin today. To be free in your own heart is not only great for you, it is great for your children and their children: it is an example that paves the way for the future happiness of entire families and society (being the conglomerate of many families). You will be doing the whole world a favour! Believe in yourself, in your power, in your discernment, in your strength and ability and in your capacity for love.

Start to live the life you want to as the person you really are and not the person everyone wants you to be. Your authentic personality is an expression of your natural sense of self, of who you truly are. I wish you joy in your life, success in your endeavours and a great deal of laughter too! Hold life lightly.

31514327R00072

Printed in Great Britain
by Amazon